Ridiculous Riddles

Ridiculous Riddles

Chris Tait
Illustrated by Mark Zahnd

STERLING

New York / London
www.sterlingpublishing.com/kids

Library of Congress Cataloging-in-Publication Data Available

STERLING and the distinctive Sterling logo are registered trademarks of Sterling Publishing Co., Inc.

Lot #:
10 9 8 7 6 5 4 3 2 1
09/10
Published by Sterling Publishing Co., Inc.
387 Park Avenue South, New York, NY 10016

© 2002 by Chris Tait

Distributed in Canada by Sterling Publishing
c/o Canadian Manda Group, 165 Dufferin Street
Toronto, Ontario, Canada M6K 3H6
Distributed in Australia by Capricorn Link (Australia) Pty. Ltd.
P.O. Box 704, Windsor, NSW 2756, Australia

Sterling ISBN 978-1-4027-7853-7

For information about custom editions, special sales, premium and corporate purchases, please contact Sterling Special Sales Department at 800-805-5489 or specialsales@sterlingpublishing.com.

For Tyler, the easy-going one, and his father, who remains
completely ridiculous.

Contents

1. Wild and Woolly

Why do tigers eat raw meat?
Because they're lousy cooks!

Of all the big cats, which one can't you ever trust?
The cheetah!

What did the cheetah say when he was accused of telling lies?
"You have to believe me! I'm not lion!"

What jungle animal is the sharpest dresser?
The dandy lion!

How do lions do their shopping?
From cat-alogues!

Why are leopards easier to see than jaguars?
Because you can always spot a leopard!

What is the most up-to-date animal in the zoo?
The gnu, of course!

What did the antelope say when he read the paper?
"That's gnus to me!"

What do you call a bear with no shoes?
Bear foot!

What kind of bike do polar bears ride?
An ice-cycle!

What did the mother kangaroo give birth to?
A bouncing baby!

HERE ARE A FEW STINKERS...

Why do people think skunks are stupid?
Because they never use good scents!

What do skunks watch after a hard day at work?
Smell-o-vision!

What do you call a greasy pachyderm?
An oiliphant!

Why are elephants so cheap?
They get paid peanuts!

What feathered creature is the most sarcastic of all flying beasts?
The mocking bird!

What bird is the most enthusiastic?
The raven!

What monkey hangs out with you and plays games?
A chum-panzee!

Where do monkeys sleep?
In ape-ricots!

What do you call a monkey who has just turned seven?
A birthday baboon!

What is the orangutan's favorite tool?
The monkey wrench!

How does the monkey symphony begin?
Ba na na na!

Why do wolves have fur coats?
Because they'd be cold in just hats!

How do rabbits toast each other?
Hare's to you!

What do you call the place where the animals rest in the desert?
Camel lot!

What do you call a camel with no humps?
Hump free!

What would you get if you crossed a pot and a bush?
A pan tree!

What did the man say when he heard the story about the giraffe's hindquarters?

"Now that's a tall tail!"

What did the buffalo say to his child when he went to work in the morning?

"Bison!"

How do you stop a wild boar from charging?

Take away its credit card!

Do minks think hunting animals is inhumane?

Fur sure!

2. Riddle Me This!

What has four legs but never stands?
  A chair!

Here's a riddle as old as the Sphinx! What has
four legs, then two, then three?
  *Man! First he crawls, then he walks, and then he walks
  with a cane!*

Why are Saturday and Sunday stronger than the rest
of the week?
  The others are all weak days!

What do you call treasure buried under your bed?
Sleeping booty!

What is the fastest growing city in Ireland?
Doublin'!

What shouldn't you ever share with your friends?
Your cold!

What starts with e and has only one letter in it?
Envelope!

What makes windows unable to see?
Blinds!

What can one not hold, two pass, and three destroy?
A secret!

What do you call a thin secret?
A wisp-er!

What gets bigger in the summer but never grows fruit?
The temperature!

Name one thing you can never tell anyone about
without making it disappear.
Silence!

Name one thing you can't hold onto for even five minutes?
Your breath!

What has two hands but can't clap?
A watch!

How do you file your taxes?
Under T!

What letter asks too many questions?
Y!

Why is it a bad idea to laugh at people when they are down?
They might get up!

Why should you always walk a mile in people's shoes before you criticize them?
Because then you'll be a mile away and you'll have their shoes!

Why did the man tell the doctor he was going bald because he was too tall?
He said that he had grown right up through his hair!

What bow never gets tied?
A rainbow!

What is the least heavy place to live?
In a light house!

The more you take, the more you leave behind – what is it?
Footprints!

Who are the fastest moving people in the world?
The Russians!

Why did the little kid cross the playground?
To get to the other slide!

What gets wet while it dries?
A towel!

Why is Alabama so smart?
Because it has more A's than B's!

What is the worst thing to make in pottery class?
Mistakes!

What works best when it clenches its teeth?
A zipper!

What becomes smaller when you add two letters?
Small!

What word is spelled wrong in every dictionary in the world?
Wrong!

When is there no room on the moon?
When it is full!

How does Christmas always end?
With an s!

What bites without using teeth?
Frost!

What gets broken without ever being held?
A promise!

How do you know cemeteries will always be popular?
Because people are dying to get in!

Why did the man mail his friend a clock?
He wanted to see time travel!

3. Wet Your Whistle!

Which fish is the most dangerous at poker?
The card shark!

What fish have the worst odor?
Smelt!

Where do down-on-their-luck fishes end up?
Squid Row!

Why are fish so easy to weigh?
They come with their own scales!

What lullaby do you sing to a fish?
"Salmon Chanted Evening!"

What do you call the smallest fishing rod at the store?
The tad-pole!

Who is always in its house, no matter where it goes?
A turtle!

What do turtles play on their day off?
Shell games!

When can bad marks get you all wet?
When they are below C level!

What do the smartest frogs say?
"Read-it, Read-it!"

What kind of music do funky fish listen to?
Sole music!

What do fish pack before they go on vacation?
Their swimming trunks!

Why shouldn't you ever cross a piranha?
Because it has a fish's (vicious) temper!

Why did the man say hello to the ocean?
Because it waved at him!

How did the ocean say goodbye to the Queen?
She got a permanent wave!

What do you call a lifesaver for a whale?
Blubber ring!

What do you call a half-witted whale?
A simple ton!

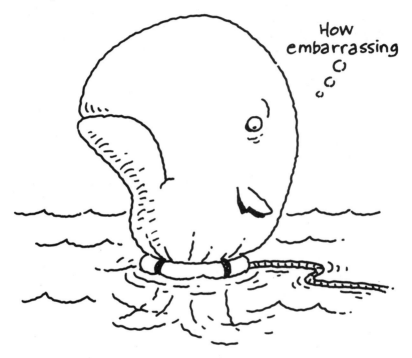

How much does it cost a pirate to get his ears pierced?
A buck an ear!

What did the creatures of the sea avoid – two by two?
Noah's shark!

Where do fishes borrow money?
At the river bank!

How did the boat know things weren't going well?
It had that sinking feeling!

Which boat is the smartest?
The scholar ship!

What did the captain say to the tired crew who was heading too far east?
"Why don't you take a little west?"

4. Sum Tricky Ones!

What did the seven dwarfs bake?
Shortbread!

Twenty sheep, a sheepdog, and a shepherd are in their favorite field. How many feet do they have?
Two! Sheep have hooves and dogs have paws!

What did Mozart become on his thirteenth birthday?
A teenager!

What snake is the best mathematician?
The adder!

Who invented the fraction?
Henry the Eighth!

What's the best way to build a computer chip?
Bit by bit!

Why are math books so hard to get along with?
They have so many problems!

What do you call it when you have to repeat a grade?
Secondary education!

Is it difficult to be impolite?
No, it's rude-a-mentary!

How can you share five apples with seven friends?
Make apple sauce!

What did the man who swallowed the dime say to his doctor?

No change yet!

You are driving a bus and three children get on at every stop for three stops. At the next two stops, two children get off. At the last stop, three children get on and one gets off. What color are the bus driver's eyes?

Look in the mirror!

What is the best time to go to the dentist?

Around tooth thirty!

Which month has twenty eight days?

They all do!

Why was the boy wearing a jacket and a raincoat to paint the fence?

He was told to put on two coats!

What is the quickest way to see your money double?

Hold it up to the mirror!

When is it not good to get a hundred on your tests?

When there are two of them!

If you have nine bowling balls in one hand
and six in the other, what do you have?
Really big hands!

If I give you six dogs today and six dogs
tomorrow and you end up with thirteen dogs,
what do you have?
A dog!

If there are two umbrellas and five people,
how can they avoid getting wet?
By going inside!

What do you get if you divide the number 8
in half?
Two 3s!

If you have two sandwiches and two sodas,
what do you have?
Lunch!

What is the difference between India and Africa?
About three thousand miles!

When is it difficult to take three teaspoons of medicine
every day?
When you only have two teaspoons!

How many seconds are in a year?
Twelve, starting with the second of January!

What kind of plants do math teachers plant?
Ones with square roots!

What are the names of the Great Plains?
747 and the Concorde!

What has four legs, one trunk, and is gray all over?
A mouse on vacation!

If there are nine flies on a table and you kill one, how many are left?
One – the others will fly away!

What can you hear and see move, but not see itself?
Wind!

What do you make bigger by taking parts away?
A hole in the ground!

What gets bigger the farther away you walk?
Your shadow!

Which is right – six and seven are twelve, or six and seven is twelve?
Neither, six and seven are thirteen!

What table has no legs?
The times table!

A family had three children, all in their teens. The first two were almost 20. How old was the last one?
Third teen!

5. Down on the Funny Farm

What animal always has a sore throat?
A horse!

How do you reward a horse that pulls your carriage on your wedding day?
With a bridle sweet!

What kind of book is *Black Beauty*?
A ponytail!

When is it all right to run without tying your shoes?
When you're a horse!

What kind of bad dream did the horse wake up from?
A night mare, of course!

What did the rider say to his unhappy horse?
"Hey, what's with the long face?"

What do you call a legless cow?
Ground beef!

What do you call a sleeping cow with horns?
A bull dozer!

What do you get from a cow after an earthquake?
A milkshake!

Why wasn't the farmer upset when he had
to share his cow with his neighbor?
Because it's no use crying over split milk!

What do you get from tiny cows?
Condensed milk!

What do you get from Arctic cows?
Cold cream!

What did the man say to the woman who put
her offspring out to pasture?
Children should be seen, not herd!

Why did the farmer take his chickens to
the vet?
It was time for their rooster shots!

What did the baby chick say about being born?
It's not all it's cracked up to be!

When is the best day to eat eggs?
Fry day!

What part of a vegetable listens best?
An ear of corn!

What loves to bite even though it only has one row of teeth?
A saw!

How do you know the porker is on his way to church?
By the pig's tie!

Why should you never tell secrets to pigs?
Because they are bound to squeal!

What did the pig think of the heat on the top of the stove?
He was bacon!

How did the farmer know his drinking water was in good health?
It was well water!

6. Say What?

Monkey starts with M and finishes with F. How is this possible?

Finishes begins with the letter F!

What antibiotic do you give a sick eraser?

Pencil-in!

What do you get when you cross cola with a bike?

A pop-sicle!

What is a hat for?

Forehead!

What do you call someone who has been hit by a meteorite?

Starstruck!

Where do you go if you get sick over the rainbow?

To the Oz-pital!

When is it okay to strike a pose?

When it hits you first!

Why should suspenders be wanted by the police?

For holding up your father's pants!

Where do criminal deer end up?

Elk a traz!

What always ends night?
T!

How does morning begin?
With an m!

What landmark has the best view?
The eye-full Tower!

What puzzle is the most dangerous to handle?
The jig saw!

What do people in Hollywood call it when they get
undressed for bed?
The sunset strip!

What do computer geeks call a horse's back?
The mane frame!

What's a semaphore?
When you can't afford a whole one!

What room is good for making baby food in?
A mush room!

Can platypuses have babies?
No, they can only have platypuses!

What do you get when you leave tangerines out in the sun?

Orange-u-tans!

How did the seven dwarfs feel when they got up in the morning?

Oh, you know – sleepy, dopey, grumpy. . .

Who would have visited the three bears if she had no hair?

Baldy locks!

Why are Santa's elves always behind in the workshop?

Because they're short-handed!

When kids are too ill to go to school, where do they feel worst?

In class!

Why are piñatas never hungry?

Because they're always stuffed!

Why did the glove fall in love?

She met someone hand some!

In the dictionary, what is the shortest month?

It's still February!

If your clock can't tell time, what should you do?

Give it a hand!

Why do pigs have pink skin?

To keep their insides in!

What is the one thing you should take before every meal?

A seat!

7. A Monstrosity of Mirth

Why do ghosts go to the opera?
  To boo the singers!

Why are ghosts so popular in class?
  They have such good school spirit!

How do ghosts learn to fight?
  By shadow boxing!

How did the ghost feel after walking home from a long night of haunting?
  Dead on his feet!

What does Godzilla look like when he gets into his bathrobe?

The kimono dragon!

What do you call a shy vampire?

Bats-ful!

What do trolls call their after-school assignments?

Gnome work!

What did the sign say above the hobbit's hole?

Gnome sweet Gnome!

Why was the monster under the bridge so funny?

He had a troll sense of humor!

What do they call the weird sisters at the beach?
Sand-witches!

How did the weird sisters get home after their brooms broke down?
They witchhiked!

What do witches' cats like for breakfast?
Sorcerers of milk!

What do witches like in their coffee?
Scream and sugar!

How did the broom meet his wife?
He swept her off her feet!

What do you call a phony wizard?
Hocus Bogus!

What is the vampires' least favorite food?
Garlic Stake!

What do waiters say when they see a ghost?
"Good evening, sir, how do you boo?"

What do you say to a self-centered giant?
"Oh, get ogre yourself!"

What did the leprechaun find after searching for the end of the rainbow at the North Pole?
A lucky pot of cold!

Why did Quasimodo stop working at noon exactly every day?

Because that's hunch time!

What kind of vegetable does Big Foot put in his garden?

Sas-squash!

Why didn't the skeleton cross the road?

He was gutless!

8. Stop Bugging Me!

industrious.
i-n-d-u-s-t...

Who are the smartest insects?
Spelling bees!

Where do insects dance?
At the moth ball!

Whom did the moth take to the ball?
An old flame!

Why was the fly so upset at the newlywed spiders?
He wasn't invited to the webbing!

What did the dot com spider say to the fly?
"Welcome to my website!"

What was the spider charged with by the bug police?
Assault with a lethal webbin!

What insect has the least courage?
The flee!

What do insects use to hold up their porches?
Cater pillars!

Who is the clumsiest bee in the hive?
The stumble bee!

What buzz can you barely understand?
A mumble bee's!

Who never makes the insect football team?
The fumble bee!

What is the bees' favorite musical?
"Stinging in the rain!"

Who is the most religious insect?
The praying mantis!

What do you say to a bug flying around your feet?
"Shoo Fly!"

What did the apple think of the worm?
It thought he was boring!

Where should you look to find out about Lyme disease?
In the tick-tionary!

9. Sports Snorts

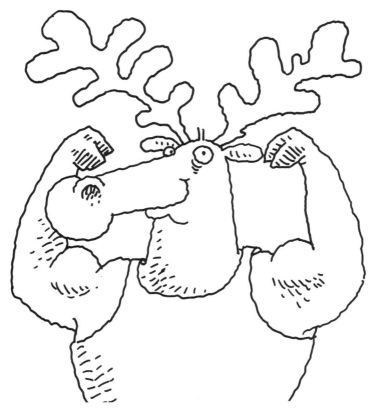

Why did the elk want a set of weights?
To work on his moose-les!

What do you call someone on the way to the gym?
Muscle bound!

What do you call a boomerang that won't come back?
A stick!

What would you get if you crossed a skater and a musician?

A hockey punk!

What do you serve a hockey player who has a cold?
Penal-tea!

What do hockey players hate most about the penalty box?

There's no elbowing room!

In hockey, which players have the best apartments?
Goalies, they have the biggest pads!

Why don't seagulls watch hockey?
It bothers them to see fowl play!

When should football players wear tuxedos?
When it's a tie game!

What is the insects' favorite sport?
Cricket!

Why was the skydiver a little nervous during
his jump?
He had that old sinking feeling!

What is harder to catch, the faster you run?
Your breath!

What did the gloomy skier say when he got off the lift?
"It's all downhill from here!"

Why did the surfer think the sea was his friend?
Because it gave him a big wave as he went by!

Why are the players so hot after a basketball game?
All the fans are gone!

What stories are told about basketball stars?
Tall tales!

What is the best hat to wear while in-line skating?
A roller derby!

What is the name of the safest German cyclist?
Helmet!

What is the name of the safest French soccer player?
Jock!

What does it say on the goalie's bumper?
The puck stops here!

What is an elephant's favorite sport?
Squash!

You win!

Why did Houdini spend so much time at the gym?
So that he'd be fit to be tied!

Where did Silly Sarah ride her bike on a snowy day?
On the slide walk!

What do you say to someone who rides his bike around in circles all day?
"One good turn deserves another!"

What do you call a slippery bike salesman?
A wheeler dealer!

Why do bikes need kickstands?
Because they're two tired!

Why did the coach have to go to the bank before the big game?

To get his quarter back!

What's the catchiest thing in baseball?

The gloves!

Where do baseball players always strike out?

The Umpire State Building!

Why are baseball players excellent bakers?

Because they make such good batters!

Why was the baseball player so proud of the cellar of his new house?

It was his first base-ment!

10. In Days of Yore

Where did Sir Lancelot go to pick up his high school diploma?
Knight school!

When did the dragon finally get full?
Around mid-knight!

What do you call a knight with no home?
A bedless horseman!

Why do dragons sleep all day?
So they can fight knights!

What do you say when you want knights to stop fighting?

"Now, joust a moment!"

What is the most interesting thing about the word knight?

It has a duel meaning.

What did the suit of armor in the museum miss most?

The knight life!

What did the suit of armor say after being left out in the rain?

"I think I'll just take a little rust!"

What did the musical animals do on Noah's boat?
They started an arkestra!

Where did Columbus land when he found America?
On the beach!

What followed the thirteenth president?
His shadow!

Why did the boy who failed history understand it the best?
Because he had to keep repeating it!

Why do archeologists have so much fun?
Because they really dig their work!

How does the archeologist sing a tune?
"Do Re Mi Fossil-ah Ti Do!"

What do you call it when a pirate digs up a scale?
Buried Measure!

Where is George Washington buried?
Underground!

11. Paws-itively Hairy!

What do cats give each other on Valentine's Day?
Chocolate mouse!

What do cats like in their drinks on hot days?
Mice cubes!

How do cats stop their favorite videos?
They put them on paws!

What did the cat say after he chased and caught the rat?

"Sorry, my mousestake!"

What do you feed a cat who yowls all night long?

Tune-a-fish!

What kind of feline can't you ever trust?

A copycat!

What did one cat say to the other cat after he saw they were being followed by a dog?

"Don't look now, but I think we're being tailed!"

What kind of dogs always get into fights?

Boxers!

Which side of a dog has the most hair?

The outside!

Which dog is the most boring?

The poo-dull!

What happened to the teddy bear who got into a fight with a dog?

He got the stuffing kicked out of him!

Where do dogs love to hang out?
In the barking lot!

What animal can always tell you the time?
A watchdog!

How does a watchdog get wound up?
He runs in circles!

What is a dog's favorite vegetable?
Pup-corn!

Where is the one place a dog can't shop?
A flea market!

What is the dog that loves to be washed?
The shampoodle!

What dog has a bark but never makes any noise?
Dogwood!

Why do cowboys love dachshunds?
They like to get a long, little doggie!

What is the best kind of animal to take on long road trips?
A car pet!

What did Hansel and Gretel's cat like most about the enchanted forest?
The gingerbread mouse!

12. Feathers, Fins, and Frogs

Where do birds invest their money?
In the stork market!

What kind of nuclear power do penguins prefer?
Ice fishin'.

What do penguins use for fishing?
The south pole!

What do you call a chicken that makes funny yolks?
A comedi-hen!

What did the little canary say when her date asked her to go dutch?

"Cheep, cheep."

What bird gulps the loudest?

The swallow!

What do ninja birds do?

Kung flew!

Heeee-yahh!

Why did the turkey cross the road?

To prove he wasn't chicken!

How do chickens learn to lay eggs?
By egg-sample!

How can a goose spend all day in the rain and not get a single hair wet?
Easily, geese don't have hair!

What do you call a class in a tree?
High school!

What did the squirrel keep locked in his trunk?
Chest nuts!

What do you call a squirrel who is crazy for chocolate?
Cocoa nut!

Why do turkeys gobble?
Because they're hungry, that's why!

How do chickens stay in shape?
With plenty of eggcersize!

Why was the newborn bird so afraid?
He was a little chicken!

What do you call a vain chicken?
Egg-o-tistical!

Why do geese fly south every year?
Because it would take them forever to walk!

How did the dodo do in school?
He graduated with extinction!

What do you say to a blue heron?
"Lighten up!"

How do you get down from an elephant?
You don't – you get down from a goose!

What has a man's name, is as small as a mouse, and wears a red jacket?
A robin!

What soda do frogs like best?
Cherry croak!

What kind of shoes do frogs wear on vacation?
Open toad sandals!

What do frogs like best about being on vacation?
The croak-o-nuts!

Where do frogs like to sit?
On toadstools!

What is the favorite bird of construction workers?
The crane!

Why are owls so much fun?
Because they're a real hoot to be around!

While the mother owl is at work, who takes care of her children?
The hoot-en-nanny, of course!

Why aren't chickens allowed to speak?
Because they use fowl language!

13. Love is a Funny Thing

What did the frog say to the princess who wouldn't kiss him?

"Warts the matter with you?"

Why are banjos the saddest instrument?

Because people keep picking on them!

Why are violins the happiest instruments?

Because everyone bows before them!

Why are hockey players such good kissers?
They know how to pucker up!

What is the perfect weather for a bride to get married?
Oh, around groom temperature!

What did the duck wear to the wedding?
A duck-seedo!

How did the duck know his wedding was expensive?
He had his bill right in front of him!

Why does everybody love bananas?
Because they're so a-peel-ing!

What did the friar get his wife for Christmas?
A monk coat!

Where did old soldiers take their wives dancing?
To the Cannon Ball!

What do you call the biggest dance of the winter?
The Snow Ball!

Edward's wife brought him into the hospital after a nasty bump on the noggin. But what she said to the doctor got him really confused. What did she say?

"My Ed hurts!"

What do you get if you kiss the monkey bars in winter?

Lip Stick!

How did the girl know that the letter was from her boyfriend?

It was in the male box!

What flowers have the longest memories?

Forget-me-nots!

14. Animal, Vegetable, or Mineral?

What do you call a snake that leads the symphony?
A boa conductor!

What subject do snakes like best in school?
Hissssstory, of course!

Why is hard to warm up to snakes?
Because they're cold-blooded!

Which burns longer, candles on a cake or candles on a table?
They both burn shorter!

What do you call a cool candle?
Wicked!

How do you make your Jack-o-lantern look like a pirate?
With a pumpkin patch!

When is a door not a door?
When it is a jar!

What do you call a song you sing on a road trip?
A car tune!

What part of a vegetable is the grooviest?
The beet neck!

What word has the most letters in it?
Mailbox!

Whose fault was the broken pavement?
Ash-fault!

What is the sickest part of a house?
The flue!

What do you call a hole that has been filled in?
A not hole!

What is the best smelling part of a rose?
The scent-er!

Why do onions make cooks cry?
I guess they're just scent-sitive!

Where do fibbers get their books?
At the lie brary!

Why would you want to make a garbage can angry?
To get him to flip his lid!

What do you call the strongest man in the world?
Whatever he tells you to!

What do thirsty people need at the hospital?
Thirst aid!

What has keys that never open locks?
A piano!

What is the coldest color of all?
Brrrrrgundy!

What do you feel when your house suddenly gets dark?
Delighted!

What is the fastest hose around?
Pantyhose – it's always running!

What ailment is the most fun to get?
Whooping cough!

What did the drum say when asked what time
the concert began?
Beats me!

What has streets and buildings but no people?
A map!

Why should you never eat the comics that come
with your gum?
They taste funny!

What flowers right under your nose?
Two lips!

What is ten people long and as strong as
ten people but ten people can't stand
on its head?
A rope!

What goes around wood but can't get in it?
Bark!

What do you draw that can never be seen?
Breath!

What is the most unhappy fruit?
Crab apples!

What kind of music do rabbits love best?
Hip hop!

How did the man keep his bunnies from multiplying?
He parted his hares!

What are you when you give away your bunny?
Hareless!

What color is a belch?
Burple!

Why do newspaper writers eat only from the middle of the ice cream cone?
Because they want the inside scoop!

Why did the boy throw away his pencil?
Because he was too easily lead!

What do you call an eager fruit?
Peachy keen!

Why are fireplaces so much fun?
Because they're grate to watch!

What did the bears call the woman who did their laundry?
Fold-i-locks!

How do you groom a Christmas tree?
With a pine comb!

What do you get when you cross a potato and a priest?
A chip monk!

15. Say, Does This Taste Funny to You?

How did the frog feel after his fifth cup of coffee?
A little jumpy!

What soup is fresh but still boring?
Chicken new-dull!

What cookie do you eat before lying down in the afternoon?
A nap snack!

What do you call someone who repairs fruit?
A peach cobbler!

Why didn't the moon eat dessert?
It was full!

What dessert should you always eat sitting down?
Chair-ee pie!

What makes you sadder the skinnier it gets?
An onion!

Where does ketchup stay before it appears in commercials?
In the dressing room, of course!

What is this the recipe for? Throw out the outside, cook the inside, eat the outside, throw out the inside.
Corn!

What is a good place to avoid if you're invited over for lunch?
The cannibals'!

Why did the man take the job at the bakery?
Because he kneaded the dough!

How did the cup and the saucer feel about the shoddy way they had been washed?

They thought it was dish-picable!

Why are peanuts named the way they are?

Because poonuts sounds too crude!

What is the worst tasting drink of the day?

Nas-tea!

How do detectives like their eggs?

Hard-boiled!

What did the potatoes say after the big vote?
"The eyes have it!"

Where do vegetables go to shop?
The stalk market!

What is gold soup made of?
Fourteen carrots!

What do you call it when you can't have dessert until after dinner?
Choco-late!

What vegetable can you blow up?
A pump-kin!

What would you be if you crossed a fruit with a dog?
Melon-collie!

What fruit asks a question?
What are melon!

How did the cheese feel after it was shredded?
It was grate-ful!

Where do baby cows go to eat lunch?
The calf-a-teria!

What's the opposite of spaghetti?
  Anti-pasto!

What kind of ring makes the maker cry?
  An onion ring!

What do you say to a sulky grape?
  "Quit your wining!"

What vegetable is named after its own recipe?
  Squash!

What is a tree's favorite soft drink?
  Root beer.

What do you call something that is brown and sticky?
A stick!

Why was the baker crying over his lost bread?
Because he kneaded it so badly!

Why did the baker taunt the bread?
To see if he could get a rise out of it!

What did the chef say about his first book?
"Baste on a true story!"

How do we know the chef is mean?
We caught him beating the eggs!

How do we know the chef is nasty?
We saw him whipping the cream!

What is a carpenter's favorite dessert?
Pound cake!

What do you call thirteen cakes that end up overcooked?
Baker's dozin'!

16. A Few Odd Jobs

What did the dentist say to the duck?

"Down in the mouth?"

What did the doctor say to the beautiful woman?

"My, you have a cute appendicitis!"

What did the newspaperman say to defend his strong views?

"Hey, I column as I sees 'em!"

How do you know the seven dwarfs are in debt?
  Because they sing, "I owe, I owe, it's off to work I go!"

How do doctors sneak up to check your heartbeat?
  With a stealthoscope!

Who do fish doctors pay attention to?
  The sturgeon general!

What did the dentist say to the liar who wouldn't show
his cavity?
  "Tell me the tooth!"

Why did the gardener think he was going nuts?
  He heard the beanstalk!

What hero delivers meals to your house?
  Supperman!

What is a boxer's favorite beverage?
  Punch!

What did the doctor tell the slumping man?
  "Watch your stoop!"

Why do performers like to visit prisons?
  They love a captive audience!

What is the dentist's favorite animal?
The molar bear!

What does the 75 kilogram butcher weigh in pounds?
Meat!

What did the plastic surgeon say to the duck?
"I'm going to have to re-bill you!"

Why did the contractor put his size 12 feet in the fresh concrete?
He wanted to make a big impression!

Why do farmers make great tailors?
Because they know how to sow!

How do you know that the funeral director has a cold?
You can tell by all the coffin!

What driver goes around in circles?
A screwdriver!

What driver puts screws in a glass-bottom boat?
A scuba driver!

Why did the zookeeper hate clothes shopping for her animals?
She couldn't get anything to fit over her hippos!

What do housekeeper rodents do?
Mousework!

What do astronomers sing in the bath?
"When you wash upon a star!"

Who marries every Sunday and still lives alone?
The priest!

Where does every locksmith want to live?
The Florida Keys!

What letter is always surprised?
G!

What kind of jewelry do climbers like?
Mountain earring!

How do you unlock the secrets of music?
With piano keys!

If you have a hole in your pocket and you take your pants to the tailor, what do you tell him you need?
Pocket change!

What kind of music do Santa's elves listen to every Christmas eve?
Wrap!

BOOM! BOOM!

Where do you go when you can't time an egg with your watch?

The second hand shop!

What time of day is a palindrome (the same forwards and backwards)?

Noon!

What song do cowboy pilots sing?

"Home, home on the plane!"

What do you say to someone who's sorry the book is over?

Don't worry, you're not riddle me yet!

INDEX